Camp Grandma®

☆Travel☆

Coloring and Activity

...Book...

By Jessica Breedlove

This Book Belongs to:

....

I am this many years old:

....

My Birthday is celebrated on:

....

My address is:

....

....

My favorite hobbies are:

....

....

Color the picture of Grandma using your colored pencils. Be sure to decorate her hat!

Grandma brings magic into the world of her campers. Her zest for life is contagious. She fills her camper's days with lots of projects and creative activities. Grandma's love of animals led her to share Camp Grandma with four animals whose mischievous personalities make Camp Grandma so much fun!

GrandMa

There are 8 words hidden in the puzzle below. See how quickly you can find all 8! You will find the answers below, but please, no peeking!

ANIMALS
CAMP
COOKIES
GRANDMA
HUGS
LOVE
MAGIC
PROJECT

```
P  R  O  J  E  C  T  S
Q  O  S  L  O  V  E  C
U  R  O  R  U  C  C  O
M  A  G  I  C  B  A  O
R  N  N  F  O  D  M  K
T  D  H  U  G  S  P  I
L  M  P  W  N  M  Z  E
M  A  N  I  M  A  L  S
```

Grandma's Little Busy Bee

GRANDMA'S MAZE

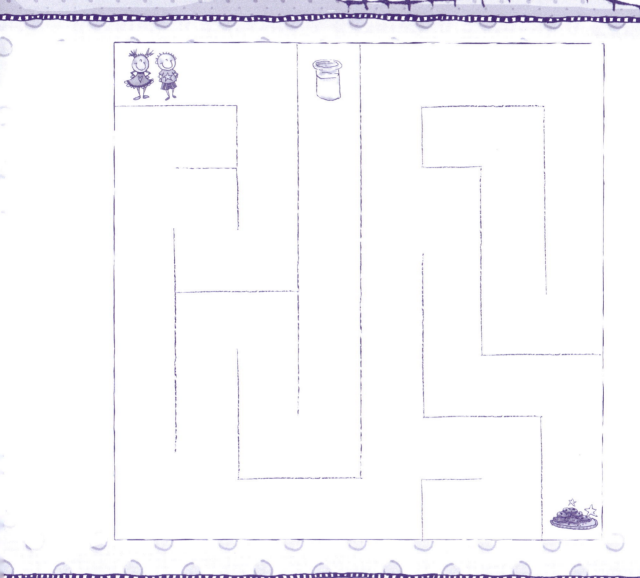

Famous for hugs & cookies

Grandma needs help finding her things. Search the picture for hidden objects.

1. MOLLY SNURTLE
2. ENVELOPE
3. LAMPSHADE
4. YELLA DUCK
5. STAR
6. PLAYHOUSE
7. LUNCH BOX
8. BABY BOTTLE
9. ROSES
10. TIPPY TOAD
11. FLAG
12. HEART
13. LADDER
14. TRUCK
15. BACKPACK
16. TEDDY BEAR

Color the picture of Grandpa's garage. Be sure to draw a picture of Grandpa working.

GRANDPA'S COLORING PAGE

Camp Grandma
Activities Director

GraNdPa

Grandpa is the Activities Director at Camp Grandma. His passion for tinkering with tools and his love for sports qualify him perfectly for this role. Grandpa is quick to laugh and loves to tell a good story.

GRANDPA'S WORD FIND

```
H A G L E S T T
D I R E C T O R
I D A C K O O U
N D N R F R L C
B P D G M Y S K
T S P O R T S J
S L A U G H U Q
A C T I V I T Y
```

ACTIVITY
DIRECTOR
GRANDPA
LAUGH
SPORTS
STORY
TOOLS
TRUCK

Zoom, Zoom!

The campers have been busy helping Grandpa. Help them pick up the tools and put them back in the workshop.

GRANDPA'S
MAZE

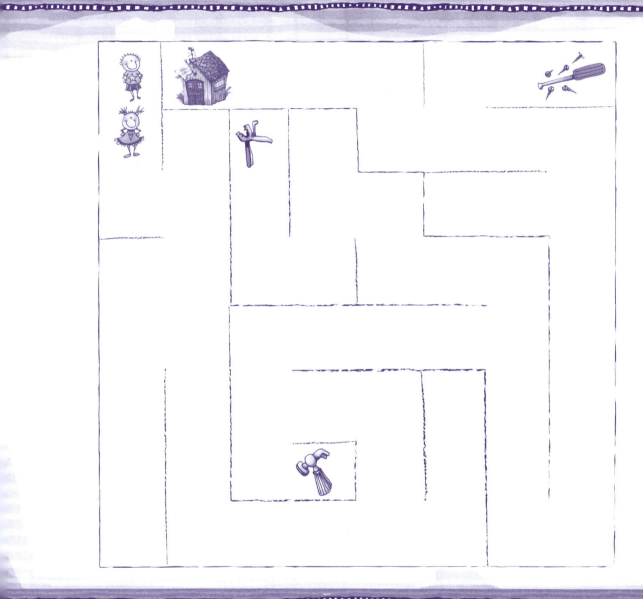

i can Fix it, too - just Like GRANDPa!

How many words can you make from the following phrase? We have given you a hint.

GRANDPA'S
WORD PLAY

Grandpa's Garage

nap

Color the picture of Yella Duck complete with his soft feathers!

Yella duck is mostly an observer. He adores participating in activities at Camp Grandma. His soft feathers protect the campers and he settles them down when they get rowdy.

Yella Duck

YELLA DUCK'S WORD FIND

There are 8 words hidden in the puzzle below. See how quickly you can find all 8! You will find the answers below, but please, no peeking!

AIRPLANE
DUCK
FEATHER
FLY
OBSERVE
SKY
SOFT
YELLOW

```
S O F T O H I O
N K E D S V X B
L P A R U E L S
U S T B D C W E
T K H C Z M K R
F Y E L L O W V
A I R P L A N E
Q F L Y S T L O
```

Visit any Season

Yella duck is going fishing, but he cannot find his hat or the night crawlers. Help him find his things and get to the car before his family leaves without him!

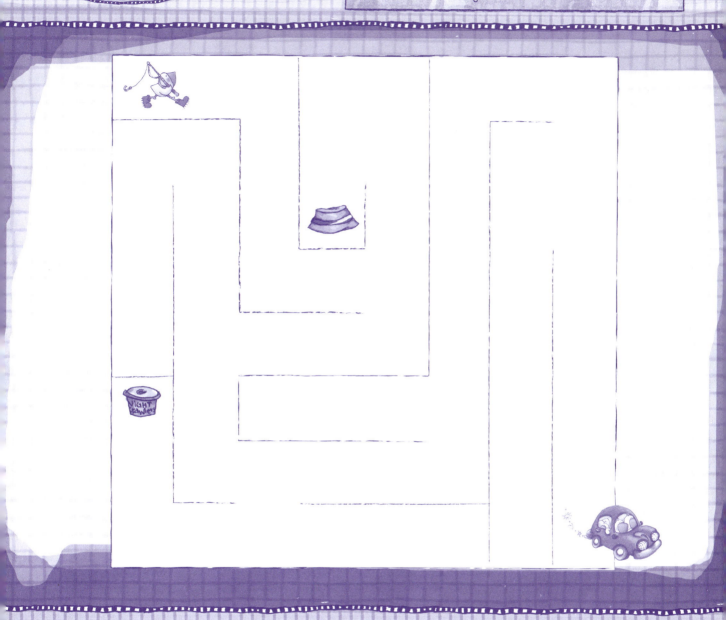

YELLA DUCK'S CAR GAMES

There are 3 different games below to keep you busy while you travel!

CRAZY ALPHABET

The object of the game is to cite all the letters of the alphabet, from a to z, using the first letter of street signs. Example Pedestrian Crossing is P.

LICENSE PLATE FUN

Watch other cars on the road and find as many license plates you can from every state you see.

SCAVENGER HUNT

See how many objects you can find while on your way to Grandma's.

AROUND THE FARM

☆ train tracks
☆ horses
☆ cows
☆ pond or lake
☆ dirt road
☆ tractor
☆ barn
☆ deer

AROUND THE CIT

☆ stop light
☆ fire hydran
☆ police car
☆ dog
☆ taxi
☆ gas station
☆ playground
☆ toy store

Molly Snurtle, in her red running shoes, zips around the playing field instructing campers on proper playing techniques and the value of practice!

Molly Snurtle

There are 8 words hidden in the puzzle below. See how quickly you can find all 8! You will find the answers below, but please, no peeking!

MOLLY SNURTLE'S WORD FIND

```
I P L A Y R M A
N R U N N I N G
S A S R Q U T S
T C O L P C G O
R T U R T L E C
U I R E O P X C
C C F D Z W L E
T E M S H O E R
```

INSTRUCT
PLAY
PRACTICE
RED
RUNNING
SHOE
SOCCER
TURTLE

Molly Snurtle is ready for a game of soccer.
Help Molly, Tippy Toad and Yella Duck meet
at the goal and make sure one of them
gets the soccer ball.

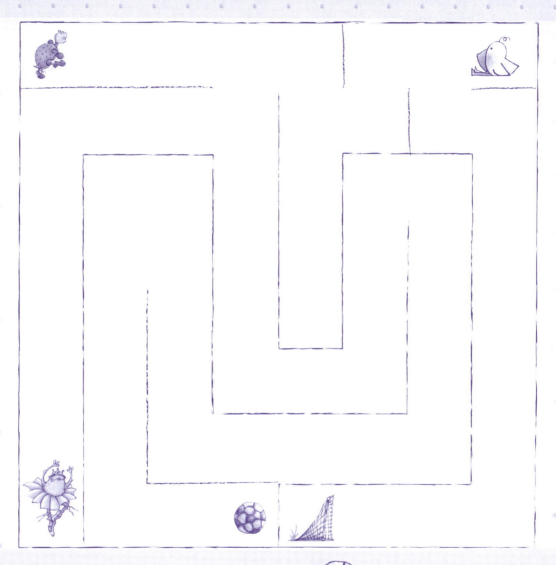

MOLLY SNURTLE'S
MAD LIB

Fill in each of the blanks with the appropriate word to complete Molly's story.

MOLLY SNURTLE'S CRAZY, MIXED-UP STORY

Fill in the blanks with the your own fun words __before__ reading the story.

Molly Snurtle loves to play .... Whenever she
                                  sport

goes to .... , she loves to bring her .... ,
            place   color

.... Every time she sees her favorite
    game   clothing

.... named .... she asks them if they
    person   silly name

want to practice on the .... together. Afterwards,
                            place

Molly always has a blast at .... where she shares her
                              fun place

.... and .... with everybody.
favorite   favorite
toy   candy

Color the picture of Plato Pig. Add more tools to the picture.

PLATO PIG'S COLORING PAGE

Plato Pig is a quiet, strong, utterly dependable sort of pig. He is Grandpa's handy helper.

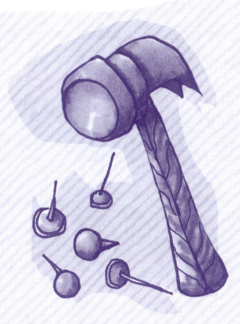

PLATO PIG'S WORD FIND

There are 8 words hidden in the puzzle below. See how quickly you can find all 8! You will find the answers below, but please, no peeking!

DEPEND
HAMMER
HANDY
HELPER
PIG
PINK
QUIET
STRONG

```
R  L  T  Z  O  T  O  J
H  A  M  M  E  R  D  S
A  E  X  Q  U  I  E  T
N  F  L  A  R  D  P  R
D  M  O  P  I  O  E  O
Y  S  P  I  E  C  N  N
L  N  U  N  F  R  D  G
O  Q  M  K  W  S  L  B
```

PLATO PIG'S MAZE

Plato Pig has been working hard all day, but Grandma has sent Yella Duck out to tell Plato it is time for dinner. Help Yella find Plato before they both miss dinner!

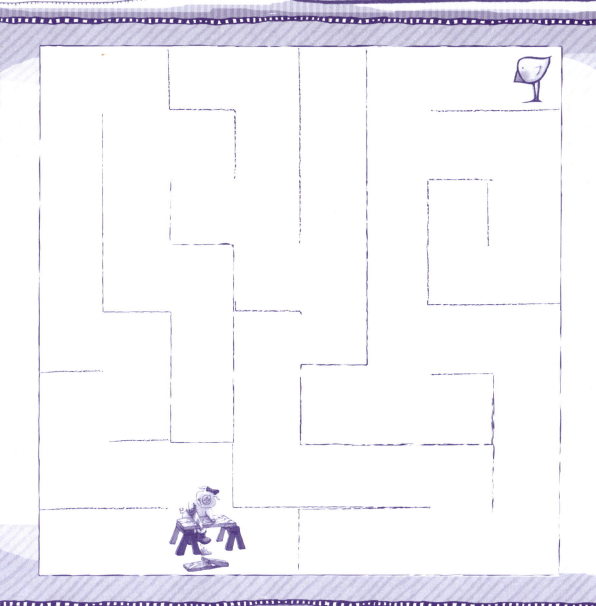

PLATO PIG'S SECRET MESSAGE

Use the code at the left side of the page to solve the secret message!

A = N
B = O
C = P
D = Q
E = R
F = S
G = T
H = U
I = V
J = W
K = X
L = Y
M = Z

T E N A Q Z N

Y B I R F

U R E   U N A Q L

U R Y C R E

C Y N G B   C V T

TIPPY TOAD'S COLORING PAGE

Color the picture of Tippy Toad. Do not forget to draw in the jewels on her crown!

Tippy Toad lives in a fantasy land where she is the Princess Ballerina. She tiptoes everywhere and brings laughter to all the campers.

There are 8 words hidden in the puzzle below. See how quickly you can find all 8! You will find the answers below, but please, no peeking!

TIPPY TOAD'S
WORD FIND

```
C R O W N F Z B
F L M T O A D A
P Q L R Q N F L
L A U G H T E L
O R E E N A M E
E S N B W S R T
T T I P P Y X N
P R I N C E S S
```

BALLET
CROWN
FANSTASY
GREEN
LAUGH
PRINCESS
TIPPY
TOAD

Tippy Toad has been out picking wild flowers. Help her gather all the flowers to take to Camp Grandma.

Help Tippy unscramble some of her favorite things by putting the words back in the correct order.

TIPPY TOAD'S WORD SCRAMBLE

HELP! TIPPY TOAD IS ALL TURNED AROUND!

1. MOEH ....

2. LLEBAT ....

3. UTTU ....

4. YLAP ....

5. NEDAC ....

6. WOCRN ....

7. ELVO ....

Answers: 1.HOME 2.BALLET 3.TUTU 4.PLAY 5.DANCE 6.CROWN 7.LOVE

The campers are busy having fun with Tippy Toad and Yella Duck. Color in the page and add some trees or maybe even a rainbow!

Camp Grandma

WORD FIND

There are 8 words hidden in the puzzle below. See how quickly you can find all 8! You will find the answers below, but please, no peeking! Be careful, this one is tricky!

AIRPLANE
BICYCLE
BOAT
BUS
CAR
TRAIN
TRUCK
WAGON

```
M  C  T  R  U  C  K  I
B  U  S  B  F  Y  H  W
I  D  G  L  O  P  X  A
C  W  R  B  Q  A  B  C
Y  A  N  I  A  R  T  A
C  G  O  E  Z  K  U  R
L  O  T  S  A  N  J  V
E  N  A  L  P  R  I  A
```

I SPY
Grandma's
TRANSPORTATION

There are many different ways for us to travel.
(any vehicle to get us to Camp Grandma is our favorite!)
Count how many different types of vehicles you can "spy" during your travels.

- Motorcycle_____
- City Bus_____
- School Bus_____
- Bicycle_____
- Mini Van_____
- Cargo Van_____
- Pickup Truck_____
- Convertible Car_____
- SUV_____
- Airplane_____
- Logging Truck_____

- Skateboard_____
- Train_____
- Blimp_____
- Boat_____
- Stroller_____
- Trolley_____
- Tractor_____
- Tricycle_____
- Big Wheel_____
- Scooter_____
- RV_____

Camp Grandma

I SPY Grandma's BUILDINGS

People live and work in buildings of all different shapes and sizes.
(But Camp Grandma is our favorite!)
How many different kinds of buildings can you "SPY" during your trip?

- ☐ Skyscraper_____
- ☐ Stadium_____
- ☐ Farm House_____
- ☐ Apartments_____
- ☐ Store_____
- ☐ Outhouse_____
- ☐ Brick House_____
- ☐ Wood House_____
- ☐ House Porch_____
- ☐ Treehouse_____
- ☐ Dog house_____

- ☐ Shed_____
- ☐ Hospital_____
- ☐ Fire Station_____
- ☐ Gas Station_____
- ☐ Resturaunt_____
- ☐ Mall_____
- ☐ Garage_____
- ☐ Barn_____
- ☐ Grocery Store_____
- ☐ Park Pavilion_____
- ☐ Car Dealership_____

How many animals on this list
can you spy?
The one who can spy the most wins.

☐ Cow _____   ☐ Turtle _____

☐ Horse _____   ☐ Fish _____

☐ Dog _____   ☐ Duck _____

☐ Cat _____   ☐ Goose _____

☐ Bird _____   ☐ Bear _____

☐ Pig _____   ☐ Moose _____

☐ Chicken _____   ☐ Hawk _____

☐ Sheep _____   ☐ Skunk _____

☐ Deer _____   ☐ Squirrel _____

☐ Rabbit _____   ☐ Beaver _____

☐ Snake _____   ☐ Fox _____

This is Tippy's favorite game! Decide who will be the x and who will be the o. Take turns with your partner drawing x's and o's until someone gets 3 in a row!

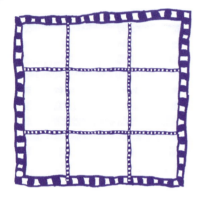
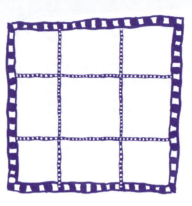
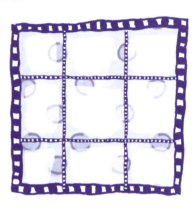

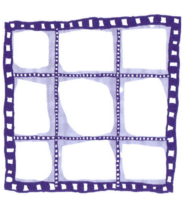
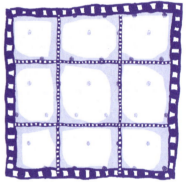

Plato Pig's workshop is full of many tools, but one very important tool is missing. Connect the dots to help Plato find his missing tool.

Camp Grandma

I WISH...

If I could invent a vehicle, it would look like...

I would let.........................ride in it.

I would paint it.............................

It would go.............................miles per hour!

draw a picture

My idea of a dream vacation is...

Activities would include...

....

....

draw a picture

When I grow up, my house will look like...

It would be located

Fill in one star or write in your own!

☆ in the mountains   ☆ on a farm

☆ on an island   ☆ in the desert

☆ in the big city   ☆ ....

draw a picture

Yella Duck has found the end of the rainbow right in Grandma's backyard and everyone is coming to see. Use the stickers to decorate the page.